The Sacred Sisterhood of
Wonderful
Wacky Women

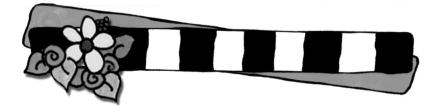

The Sacred Sisterhood of
Wonderful
Wacky Women

Suzy Toronto

Blue Mountain Press™
Boulder, Colorado

Library of Congress Catalog Card Number: 2012004136
ISBN: 978-1-59842-672-4 (previously ISBN: 0-9774956-0-4)

Wonderful Wacky Women®
Inspiring•Uplifting•Empowering

is a trademark of Suzy and Al Toronto. Used under license.

Blue Mountain Press is registered in U.S. Patent and Trademark Office.
Certain trademarks are used under license.

Printed in the United States of America.
First printing of this edition: 2012

♻ This book is printed on recycled paper.

Library of Congress Cataloging-in-Publication Data

Toronto, Suzy.
    The sacred sisterhood of wonderful wacky women / by Suzy Toronto.
        p. cm.
    ISBN 978-1-59842-672-4 (hard cover)
    1. Women–Poetry. I. Title.
    PS3620.O5886S23 2012
    811'.6–dc23

                                                                            2012004136

Blue Mountain Arts, Inc.
P.O. Box 4549, Boulder, Colorado 80306

This book is dedicated to Candy Swanson, who touched my life in ways I cannot find words to describe... who refused to let me be anything less than myself... and who loved me like no friend ever has.

Table of Contents

Introduction 9

Why No Faces? 13

They Who Are Best Friends 15

She Who Is a Mother............................... 21

She Who Is a Wonder of a Woman.......................... 37

She Who Has a Great Attitude................................ 43

She Who Loves the Beach......................... 51

She Who Stands for Something.............................. 57

She Whom I Lean On 63

They Who Are Sisters............................... 69

She Who Loves to Grow Stuff 77

She Who Gives of Herself........................ 83

She Who Seeks a Better Way................... 89

She Who Has Arrived............................... 99

Okay, so... this is me!

Here I am, painting on my back porch, doing what I love most. When I'm not at an art show or sitting on the beach, this is where you'll find me, working on a new idea or project that kept me awake the night before.

I come by art naturally. I am the daughter of an artist, who is the daughter of an artist, who is the daughter of an artist. It is in my blood. All the education in the world cannot infuse that kind of bloodline into someone, and I feel blessed to have this legacy of women behind me. I don't remember not knowing how to draw, mold, shape, or create anything. From my fine art that hangs in galleries to the variety of whimsical characters in my commercial lines, I am always exploring new ways to express the energy inside me. I feel forever blessed to have these gifts and vow to never take them for granted.

I am now smack in the middle of my "fifty-somethings," living in Tangerine, Florida, in a funky house surrounded by hundred-year-old oak trees. I share that space with my husband, Al, and my precious dog, Lucy. I eat chocolate truffles while I paint, and when they run out, I quit. I drink so much Perrier sparkling water I'm considering buying stock in the company. I practice yoga, which for some strange reason I think will help compensate for my horrible diet, and I go to the beach every chance I get.

I have five grown children and twelve grandkids who love me as much as I adore them. I've taught them to dip their French fries in their chocolate shakes, to make up any words they want to any tune they like, and to never, ever color inside the lines.

Aloha,

Suzy

Introduction

When I hear the words "families are forever," I sometimes wonder if it's a curse or a blessing. Don't get me wrong, I'm heavily bonded to my children, sister, mom, dad, and husband… but the fact is, I didn't choose any of them.

(I know you're thinking I chose my husband, but I have to admit, I was under the influence of raging hormones at the time… and he was just about the most irresistible, little old thing I'd ever laid eyes on! I really had no choice.)

But do I really want all my family in my life forever? Well, of course I do! The concept of an eternal family is the cornerstone of my belief system, although there have been days when I seriously doubted whether I wanted any of them. Some days are just like that. When I hear the phrase "families are forever," what I really wonder is, are friends forever too?

If not, just stop the world and let me get off!

I am a "girlfriend" kind of girl. Not every woman is—but a lot of us are. I love having girlfriends in my life. The thought of picking up the phone and not having my dear, sweet friends

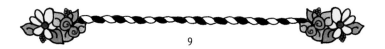

on the other end to talk to, cry to, and visit with is simply unbearable for me. I won't even get into going shopping, doing lunch, or getting pedicures—things that for me absolutely necessitate the presence of a girlfriend. When I think about women who claim to not need a girlfriend in their lives, I figure they just haven't found a good one yet. I do not have that problem. I have been blessed with an abundance of the most wild, wacky, wonderful women God ever created to be my friends.

This is a blessing I do not take lightly.

When I drew the first of my Wonderful Wacky Women, I had no idea the series would blossom into the success it is today. I believe the appeal of my work comes from the images and stories of real women. I simply paint and describe my wacky group of friends. For, you see, I am surrounded by ordinary women who have accomplished extraordinary things. It is about these unrecognized feats of quiet, female heroism that I write.

I simply pour out my heart on paper while holding a paintbrush in my hand. I am often caught with tears streaming down my face—not tears of sadness or pain, but tears of joy—as I write about the power of womanhood and the enormous variety of relationships women have with one another. These relationships outlast the toughest of times and become strengthened beyond measure. They are the kind of friendships that make up the very fabric of our lives. They truly have the power to create a better tomorrow.

Who are these wonderful, wacky women? You know them. They are your friends, your sisters, your mothers, and your grandmothers. They are even you and me! They are the women who rise above all obstacles to turn tragedy into triumph and who answer the call to make a difference in the world.

It is with profound joy that I introduce a few of these remarkable women to you now.

Why No Faces?

The Wonderful Wacky Women concept began well over a decade ago with my eight-year-old son who is adopted. One day he innocently asked, "Mommy, who is she that grew me in her tummy?" Wanting to answer, but not knowing much, I replied, "I'll draw you a picture of her." I sketched out "She Who Is with Child," which I patterned after myself, right down to my untamed hair and bare feet. I wanted him to think he was no better off and no worse off—he was just with the mom God wanted him to have. I left the character faceless to allow him to imagine what she looked like. It satisfied him, and he went on with his child's play.

Today, over two decades later, my son, Chase, is my biggest fan. Since that day, so many years ago, The Sacred Sisterhood of Wonderful Wacky Women, who stand for all that is good and right in the world, has captured the imagination of millions.

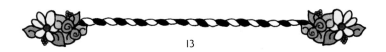

They Who Are Best Friends

You laugh when people ask
if you're sisters…
you're so much closer than that!
She knows everything about you,
all your secrets… all your quirks…
all your insecurities and struggles.
She also knows the silly things…
all the things that make you goofy.
And she loves you anyway.
You've shared with her things
you'd never tell another living soul!
She's your companion, your conscience,
and your confidante.
She's your critic and
the president of your fan club
all rolled into one.
She's the friend
you've always prayed for.
And now you're blessed beyond measure…
for she is your best friend!

They Who Are Best Friends

I love having girlfriends. I've been blessed by such an abundance of different women in my life, I can't figure out if God loves me so much that he graced me with this honor or He figures I'm so messed up I need all the help I can get. Most likely, it's the latter—because I have lots of girlfriends.

I have beach friends and shopping friends… yoga friends, diet friends, and art friends… phone friends, church friends, and neighbor friends. There are friends I can call on the spur of the moment for a "wild, wacky women" vacation and others with whom vacations require months of planning. I have friends to learn from and friends to lean on… friends to laugh with and friends to cry with.

Then—apart from all the rest—I have Candy.

I often find myself using the present tense when speaking of Candy, even though she died of ovarian cancer in July 2003. I feel her presence continually. I'm still stuck in the "denial" phase of the grieving process. But, hey, so far it's working for me!

Candy is the inspiration for so much of my work. There is no other person in my life, save my mother, whose life has so influenced me to reach beyond myself.

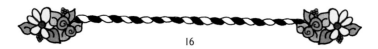

Candy and I met in 1984, half a world away in a rundown little hotel in Tel Aviv, Israel—a block away from the Mediterranean Sea. We had independently signed up for a tour of the Holy Land. We were linking up with other members of the group to spend several weeks exploring the rich history of this ancient land. Our by-chance meeting blossomed six years later when I moved to Coeur d'Alene, Idaho—Candy's hometown. My inescapable draw toward her changed me forever. The woman, the artist, and the author I am today is due, in part, to her.

Best girlfriend-to-girlfriend relationships are so precious. They fill a need within us that all other relationships lack. As close as you might be to other men and women, until you have truly experienced such a sacred girl-to-girl connection, you won't understand. Men never will. Both Candy's husband and mine quit trying to understand. They just accept it at face value.

There was an indescribable closeness between Candy and me—a comfort level I have never had with any other friend. I could start a thought, and she'd finish it. I never had to explain or excuse myself. She knew where I came from and where I was going. When I got off track, she'd lovingly nudge me back on. When I resisted, she'd chew me out!

It's interesting that my most cherished memories of Candy are silly ones—memories that to most people won't seem significant or profound. But in my mind, they define our friendship.

One such incident happened on a beautiful fall morning. I was in the back bedroom of my house, blow-drying my hair. When I turned the blower off, I could hear my cat meowing every few seconds, followed by a woman's voice. At first I thought it was the TV, but it wasn't. It was Candy. Tired and overwhelmed by her strict macrobiotic diet—an attempt to eradicate the cancer in her body—she needed a break. She was craving ice cream, and she knew I'd have some. I'm a mint-chocolate-chip ice cream junkie.

There she was—her thin, frail body sitting at my kitchen bar with a whole half gallon of Breyers ice cream and a spoon. She had coaxed Bob, my twenty-eight-pound cat, to jump up on the kitchen bar next to her. Together, they were sharing bites of ice cream directly out of the carton—yes, both of them! In a very matter-of-fact tone, she was explaining to Bob that she wasn't as fond of the chocolate chips as she was of the ice cream itself. So she was spitting the chips out into a neat, little pile next to him. He batted them around the bar and amused her as she nibbled on the cool, decadent ice cream that was so taboo.

As I peeked around the corner, I was first struck by the thought that if one of my kids had been doing this, I would have hollered, "Knock it off," even though I've been known to steal a few bites out of the carton myself. Yet seeing my dear, precious Candy commit this very same act overwhelmed me with a sense of warmth. I was so blessed to have a friend who felt such irrepressible comfort and familiarity with me that she could—without even asking or announcing her presence—

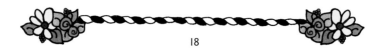

walk in and truly make herself at home. I left them to their binge and never said a word. Like I said, it's silly, but it's a lasting memory I will always cherish.

My heart and mind are filled with the wit and wisdom of my dear friend. Sometimes I miss her so much it overwhelms me. But I feel blessed beyond words to have been given the chance to have her in my life. My greatest honor is that she chose me as her best friend too.

Suzy's Mint-Chocolate-Chip Ice Cream with Fudge Sauce

One jar of Dove fudge sauce, one half gallon of Breyers mint-chocolate-chip ice cream, and two very long-handled ice-tea spoons

Directions:
1.   Call your best friend and invite her over. While she is en route, grab a spoon and eat a well out of the center of the half-gallon container.

2.   Dump the jar of fudge into the well.

3.   Get two long-handled ice-tea spoons ready. (They're more fun to eat with.)

4.   When your friend arrives, tell her how much you love and appreciate her, swear her to secrecy, and then dive in. Remember, calories don't count if you don't tell anyone.

5.   Laugh, cry, talk—and have a bite for me.

She Who Is a Mother

"She Who Is with Child" is my very first Wacky Woman.
It deals with the joys and sorrows of pregnancy. But my
view of motherhood needs to be viewed in the context
of my total experience to be appreciated, so I've put it
all together in this chapter. The following pages contain
five images and poems. The first two are about biological
children, followed by "She Who Is a Birth Mother," a
tribute to the woman who bore my adopted son. And
though somewhat redundant with the other stories, "She
Who Is an Adoptive Mother" is an expression of my
feelings upon receiving my boy. Last but not least, "She
Who Is a Foster Mother" describes another blessing in
my life. Then I tie these all together with my own history
of motherhood.

She Who Is a Mother

A miracle occurred when the infant
was first laid in her arms.
She was transformed from a woman
into a goddess known as "Mother."

She thought she'd known
the depths of love.
She thought she'd seen
the heights of success.
She thought she'd experienced
that which is true joy.
But nothing compared to this.

All else faded when her baby
drew its first breath
and she became a co-creator with God.

She Who Is with Child

Some women are just made
for birthin' babies.
For others, it's a sacrifice.
She Who Is with Child knows that
she is a co-creator with God.
The nausea comes and goes...
the kicking may last all night...
the last month may be torture...
but then she hears
that still, small voice:
"I know it's not easy now,
but soon it will all be worth it."

She Who Is a Birth Mother

She carries within her a precious, precious life…
one that empowers her to give the unparalleled gift of
motherhood to another woman.

The choice is not easy.
Such monumental decisions seldom are.
The conflict in her heart tugs back and forth
as she struggles to let go.
Will her child really be better off?

She closes her eyes
and lifts her face toward heaven…
and she says a silent prayer.

Then she catches the vision of a family—
a mom, a dad, grandparents,
aunts, uncles, and cousins—
all weeping with joy over this treasured infant…
the newest member of their family…
the miracle they thought they'd never see.

She softly begins to cry.
With a breaking heart and perfect clarity of mind,
a still, small voice
whispers her thundering decision…
"It will not be easy,
but it is right."

She Who Is an Adoptive Mother

A miracle occurred when the infant
was first laid in her arms.
She was transformed from a woman
into a goddess known as "Mother."

For so many years,
she had stifled the pain of empty arms,
believing this moment would never come.
So she focused elsewhere on making a
difference in the world,
seeking fulfillment as best she could.

But now a newborn baby lay in her arms.

She thought she'd known the depths of love…
she thought she'd seen the heights of success…
she thought she'd experienced true joy.
But nothing compared to this.
All else faded when she gazed into
the face of the miracle
she thought could never be hers…
a child to call her own.

She Who Is a Foster Mom

When she first considered becoming a foster mother,
her first thought was…
"Sure, what's another potato in the pot?"
But opening her home to children
who had nowhere else to go
enveloped her with new emotions.

She soon realized that each one came
with his or her own unique set of challenges.
Scared and alone,
these children carried emotional baggage
that molded their behavior and dared her to get close.

But "get close" she did!
She rejoiced at their progress
and wept at their setbacks.
Despite sometimes being pushed away, she pressed on…
trying to make a difference, one child at a time.

What she was totally unprepared for was
the tremendous love she developed for these children.
Whether she had them for a few days or a few years,
she left a loving imprint on each one's heart.

Now when people ask
how many children she has, she hesitates…
Originally? Currently? Or altogether?
Over the years, they've all been hers…
and a part of them always will be.

My Motherhood

As a young woman, I was diagnosed with endometriosis, a disease that at the time caused infertility in women about 80 percent of the time. My disease progressed from bad to worse, and at the age of twenty-three, I had one of those experiences you only see in the movies where a person goes to bed feeling a little under the weather and opens her eyes the next morning in a hospital recovery room without the slightest idea how she got there.

I awoke in tremendous pain, having undergone emergency surgery in the middle of the night. Groggy from the medication, I tried to clear my head and saw a doctor standing at the foot of my bed. He told me I would *never* have a child. The date will forever remain clear in my mind: May 10, 1981, Mother's Day. I started to cry but quickly stopped as my deep sobs only intensified the pain. It was easier to hold in what I was feeling and give in to the drug-induced sleep.

"Never have a child" rang through my mind. Who was this stupid man to tell me I would never have a child? Maybe never give birth, but never have a child? I didn't like his choice of words, and someday I'm going to tell him. I decided to take it as a challenge. Not only would I have children, but I was determined to have a

whole houseful of them. With the help of a nurse at the hospital, I started the adoption process the very next day, making that first phone call from my hospital bed.

Eighteen months later, a beautiful baby boy was placed in my arms. I couldn't believe it. I was overwhelmed with emotion. I was awed by the fact that a woman I did not know was willing to give me the opportunity to be a mother. The most precious gift anyone could ever receive was wrapped in a blue flannel blanket, screaming his little, itty-bitty head off! As I held *my* son in *my* arms, I sobbed. This time they were tears of complete joy. I was a mother at last— an adoptive mother, yes, but a mother nonetheless. My life would never be the same.

Four years later, I embarked on a new kind of motherhood. I was divorced and a single mom. Although it was tough, I still embraced my role as a mother. I adored my son and lived for him. Even though I had to divide my time between being a mother and being a working girl, I was focused and determined to create a fun and exciting life for the two of us. And I did just that.

The dream of having a large family was still in the back of my mind, and I was not about to give up. I've always believed that I have the ability to create any kind of life I want. That's when I met Al Toronto, a handsome widower with four children. His wife had recently died after a four-year battle with breast cancer. He was lonely and wanted to remarry. He was equally desperate for a mother for his four children. I saw the opportunity and jumped right in. It was easy—jumping in, that is. Al was just about the

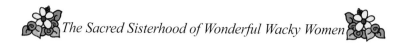

cutest thing I'd ever seen, and I fell helplessly, hopelessly, head-over-heels in love with him and the kids. I sold my business, gave up my career, and became a full-time homemaker, wife, and mother—this time adding "step-mother" to the list.

If that wasn't enough, shortly after our marriage we became aware of a young Native American girl from the Navajo tribe who needed a home. Brenda joined our family, and I added "foster mother" to the list.

To make a long story short, I was twenty-nine years old with six kids, all calling me "Mom." I had refused to accept the "no child" prognosis that was handed to me. I dreamed up a new one and made it happen. Today, almost thirty years later, all my children are grown and on their own. Together they have blessed me with twelve grandkids. Like my children, none of them have my blood coursing through their veins, but they each carry a piece of me through their parent's upbringing. They are my posterity, and I am their legacy. Of this there is no doubt.

Never have a child? Ha! That doctor really was a stupid man. I wish he could see me now.

Suzy Toronto

Chase's Tortilla Soup

This is my son's favorite meal. He discovered it while working on the Navajo reservation in Arizona. When I first saw this recipe, I told Chase I didn't think it was going to be that great. But he prodded me to fix it and follow the recipe exactly as outlined below. Wow, was it wonderful! Now, every time I fix it, I get rave reviews, and Chase just gives me a knowing smile.

2 cups cooked chicken meat, cut into pieces
1 onion, chopped
1 teaspoon olive oil
2 4-ounce cans chopped green chilies
1 teaspoon fresh garlic, minced
1 teaspoon ground cumin
½ teaspoon dried oregano
½ teaspoon ground red pepper
¼ cup green onion, chopped
1 15-ounce can Northern white beans, undrained
For garnish: sour cream, avocado slices, and sliced green onions

In a large pot, sauté onion in olive oil. Add remaining ingredients except for the beans. Cook for 20 minutes on low, letting it simmer and fill the house with the most amazing aroma. Add beans and cook for another 5 minutes to heat through.

Top with a dollop of sour cream, an avocado slice, and green onions. Ooooh, just writing down this recipe makes me hungry. I'm going to fix some right now.

She Who Is a
Wonder of a Woman

No matter what you ask of her,
the answer is always the same…
a resounding "YES!"

And her word is as good as gold.

With her sink-or-swim attitude,
she tackles any assignment,
jumping in with both feet
and working like crazy to learn,
implement, and complete the task.

It doesn't matter
that she's never done it before.
Her motto is "Fake it till you make it,"
and it appears to everyone that
she can do anything.

She devotes her time and energy
to everyone she meets,
and her talents multiply exponentially.

She is the personification of a "can do" girl…
the epitome of
female power and intelligence…
a true wonder of a woman!

She Who Is a Wonder of a Woman

The absolute wackiest girl I know is Launi, and she is incredible.

My friendship with Launi began shortly after my friend Candy was diagnosed with ovarian cancer. In an effort to find cute hats and wigs to cover her chemo-related baldness, Candy and I started a company called Perfect Solutions. We offered a variety of products to women who were enduring the rigors of chemotherapy. I had designed a dozen hats with detachable human-hair bangs. We called the line "It's Me Again." The demand for the hats was wonderful, and before we knew it, we had wholesale accounts and individual orders pouring in. We needed help. We were looking for a general office manager who could oversee the business and accounting. My time was devoted to production, and Candy's time was spent on marketing—not to mention coping with her own therapy. Launi convinced us she was our girl, and we hired her on the spot.

Besides the fact that she seemed to have all the skills we needed to run the office, Launi made Candy laugh. I call her hysterical antics a "Launi fix." They were a godsend at a

time when Candy's life was largely doomed to chemotherapy, hospitals, and doctors. Bringing a healthy dose of laughter into our lives at that time was worth twice what we paid her.

We dumped all our administrative work on Launi. We handed her the unopened accounting computer software we had purchased, the raw goods inventory files, the accounts receivable and payable, and a handful of shipping orders. A huge burden was lifted from our shoulders as she walked out the door with the box of papers and software. We knew it was in good hands.

Launi, on the other hand, was in a sheer panic. She raced home, got out a dictionary, and starting looking up the term "A-c-c-o-u-n-t-s R-e-c-e-i-v-a-b-l-e." Then she called her son to ask him how to turn on the computer. Over the next three weeks she got to know the tech support people at QuickBooks on a first-name basis. She somehow managed to get private lessons by calling them at 2:00 a.m. and asking one question at a time until she knew as much as they did. She claims this education is responsible for the extra ten pounds she gained in the course of our friendship. While on hold for what seemed like hours, she'd nibble on anything chocolate throughout the night. Her excuse was that the caffeine in the chocolate helped keep her awake. (Yeah, right!) Anyway, she made up her own system to get things organized, paid invoices as she received them, and had the whole business up and running efficiently in no time. Candy and I were thrilled. Over the next couple of years, unbeknownst to either of us, this same sink-or-swim

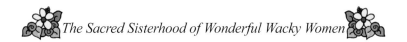
scenario played out over and over again with Launi. We just kept piling on the work. By the time we sold the business, Launi had taught herself everything she needed to know to run the office. Not only did she get us by, but she did an outstanding job.

As I reflect on all this, I wonder how often in life I have let the minor fact that I didn't know how to do something hold me back. Now when those moments hit me, I call my dear friend and get a quick "Launi fix." She can kick-start me into a "fake it till you make it" mode in no time at all. With her encouragement, I jump into any pot of hot water and learn how to swim on the way out.

I have known Launi for about twenty years. She has grown into a remarkable woman with true skills that can rival anyone's. And it's still amazing to see her in action. But here's the thing: it's actually kind of fun to call her up in the middle of the night and ask her if she can do some wild, harebrained task just to see if she can figure it out. And you know what? It's not always conventional—but she pulls it off every time.

She is, truly, a wonder of a woman.

Suzy Toronto

Launi's Wonder-of-a-Woman Way
to Start the Day

Drag yourself out of bed, drive to Mimi's Cafe, and order "Pain Perdu." Don't get the whole breakfast, just a side order for $3.49. It's sort of a French-toast sandwich thingy, stuffed with cream cheese and orange marmalade. While you're waiting for your Pain Perdu, ask the waiter to bring you a large mug of hot chocolate with extra whipped cream. For some reason, the hot chocolate is especially good here.

Or if you've had a long night on hold with "tech support," sleep till noon, drive to Panda Express, and order Orange Chicken.

Either way, enjoy yourself. And for goodness sake, try not to waddle on your way out the door!

She Who Has a Great Attitude

The way she sees it,
if you want rainbows,
you gotta have rain.
So she pulls up her bootstraps
in the storm
and goes out looking
for puddles to play in.
She brightens up every dark place…
selflessly lifting, soothing, and serving.
She finds joy in the journey
in both the hills and valleys…
and just about everything
makes her laugh!
For her,
laughter in the face of adversity
is the finest sound there is.
She has a great attitude!

She Who Has a Great Attitude

Ding-a-ling-a-ling… Hello? Chit-chat, chit-chat… Yadda, yadda, yadda… Laugh, laugh, giggle, snort… "Oh, by the way, did I tell you I have breast cancer?"

That's how I found out my friend Carrie had been diagnosed with stage II breast cancer.

Carrie and I met over a decade ago. I signed up for one of her adult watercolor classes through the adult education program at our local college. I was in one of those "I gotta do something fun or this dreary north Idaho winter weather is gonna drive me stark raving mad" moods. I did not choose this class because I needed to explore the medium of watercolor, but rather because the program had the word "adult" in the title. I was desperate to have a meaningful conversation with anyone who didn't call me "Mom."

I walked into the room, and there, standing at the head of the class, was a wild, wacky woman. Her looks, voice, and mannerisms personified the description of a free-spirited

artist living in the woods of northern Idaho. Part mountain mama, part drama queen, Carrie was an extraordinary enigma that defied all description. Paint was flying, she was barking out instructions, and everyone in the room was laughing hysterically. I smiled. I knew this was just what I needed.

Aside from teaching, Carrie is one of this country's most accomplished forensic artists. Her credentials and career are enough to knock your socks off. She is sought out by law enforcement agencies to help identify some of this country's most elusive criminals. She is the author of numerous books, ranging from technical manuals to juicy novels based on some of her most celebrated cases. Add to that her mastery of the medium of watercolor and her over-the-top teaching skills, and you get a glimpse of how lucky I was to be in this class.

And she didn't often teach. But that winter she'd gotten the itch to drop what she was doing and teach this class of misfit, middle-aged, wannabe artists just for the fun of it. You see, Carrie loves to teach, and when she does, she teaches every trick she knows, holding nothing back.

During that dreary winter in northern Idaho, I was totally unprepared for the brightness of her off-the-wall sense of humor. Her upside-down perspective on life, the universe, and everything else totally caught me off-guard—something that is not easily done. As each class began, I could hardly decide if I was sitting in the most wonderful technical and creative art class I had ever taken or a standup comedy club.

By the end of the class, Carrie and I had developed a lasting relationship of mutual respect and collaborative laughter. Although we now lead very different and busy lives, our spur-of-the-moment, out-of-the-blue phone calls to each other use up way too many minutes on our cell phones. Those calls, which always start with a simple question, last for hours. Topics range from insightful, philosophical discussions to humorous, silly girl talk. All our calls, however, are filled with laughter. This woman can make me laugh so hard my sides ache for an hour after hanging up. I always smile when I see her number pop up on my caller ID. I know before I answer that I'm going to have a good time.

When she dropped the bomb on me that she had been diagnosed with breast cancer, I was stunned. Too many of my friends had fallen prey to cancer. One had recently died, and I was not prepared for another. It was at this moment that Carrie's true character began to show itself to me. She told me about the doctor who found the lump in a routine mammogram. Neither she nor the doctor ever felt a lump, but it was there nevertheless. After a round of biopsies, a positive diagnosis was made. The doctor was obviously uncomfortable being the bearer of bad news, as he awkwardly told her that her right breast would have to be removed. Sensing his discomfort, Carrie quickly consoled him and exclaimed, "It's okay, Doc, really! I have another one just like it on the other side."

As we talked about her treatment and recovery, I asked about

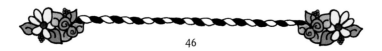

her hair. When my dear friend Candy was going through chemotherapy, I made special hats for her, which led to our starting a company called Perfect Solutions that specialized in headwear for women going through cancer. I was hoping to help Carrie out with some of my hat designs. I somberly offered my services, and she quickly broke into laugher. She was not upset at all that her head would be completely bald. In fact, she was thrilled that her whole body would be void of hair everywhere. "Yay, no more shaving," she bellowed.

Carrie's doctor was also concerned that, like most women, she might have serious issues and stress with hair loss. He tried to comfort her by saying, "Not to worry, Carrie. All your hair will come back, and when it does, it will be twice as thick and curly as ever."

"Oh great," she exclaimed. "That means I'm gonna have armpits that will make me look like a member of the Czechoslovakian shot-put team!"

Carrie jumped into the recovery process as if it were a new adventure. With an attitude that every woman hopes she will have but doesn't really believe she can muster, Carrie never doubted for a second that she would completely recover. The only real question was how much mileage she could get out of it and how many jokes she could glean from it all. (Remember that teeny-tiny bit of drama queen in her?) She was determined to learn whatever lessons God had in store for her and come out a better person for having experienced them, which was exactly

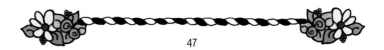

how she tackled every other problem in her life.

Carrie continued to work, teach, and paint all through her treatments, and she's now in full remission and feeling fine. As for me, I'm not doing so great. I'm still doubled over from laughing too hard.

As I think about the depth, richness, and, yes, the laughter Carrie has brought to my life, I smile. I don't think she has a clue of the profound impact she has made on me, my art, and my career. It is with great admiration that I share her with you here, for I feel blessed beyond measure to have her as a friend.

It's not only her shining example of how to survive, but more so her ability to really LIVE every minute of her life with fun, energy, and humor that, without exception, makes Carrie "She Who Has a Great Attitude."

Thanks, Carrie, for teaching me which end of the brush to get wet.

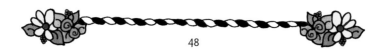

Suzy Toronto

French Silk Chocolate Headache

Carrie and I decided to skip lunch one day while at a workshop and split a piece of this decadent dessert instead. Forty-five minutes later, all that richness in our empty stomachs gave us both splitting headaches. We decided it was worth every bite!

Oreo cookies
1 prepared 8-inch pie shell, baked
½ cup (1 stick) unsalted butter
¾ cup sugar
1 ounce (1 square) unsweetened chocolate, melted and cooled
1 teaspoon vanilla
2 large eggs
For garnish: whipped cream and pecans

Smash up enough Oreo cookies to fill the bottom of the baked pie shell, pressing them firmly into the bottom. You don't need to add anything else because the frosting between the wafers will hold it all together.

In a small bowl, cream the butter and sugar with an electric mixer until very light and fluffy—the longer you beat it, the better. Mix in chocolate and vanilla until blended. Now add eggs one at a time: beat the first one at medium speed for 5 minutes; then add the second one and beat for an additional 5 minutes. Do not cut this step short. Dump the whole mixture into the prepared crust. Chill for 2 hours. Top with whipped cream and pecans. (We like nuts on everything.)

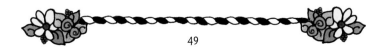

She Who Loves
the Beach

No words can express
the depth of her contentment
as she walks along the beach.
As the waves lap against the shore,
they create the rhythm of her life.
Balmy breezes kiss
her sun-bronzed skin,
and she wonders…
could there ever be a greater destiny
than to be born with a love
for the treasures of the sea?
Here, she is home.

She Who Loves the Beach

Few things bring me more joy than being at the beach. Growing up in Hawaii, I learned early on that the ocean, with its power and vastness, would forever become a focal point of my life.

I love everything about the beach. I love the salty air and the texture of the sand. My heart beats with the rhythm of the waves, and my life cycles with the flow of the tides. I am awestruck by the power the sea has to both bring forth life and then, just as easily, take it away.

Although I now live far from my beloved islands, I sneak off to Florida's sunny beaches every chance I get. As a matter of fact, this very minute I am sitting on the beach, toes curled in the sand, waves breaking at my feet, typing on my laptop. I have always believed life is what you make it. Today, I'm making it the beach.

I'd like to claim that I'm the original "She Who Loves the Beach," but I'm not. That title belongs to one of my aunts—a wild, wacky, wonderful woman named Clover. Clover lives in

the Port of the Islands in the Florida Everglades—the entrance to the chain of Ten Thousand Islands. From her home on the water, Clover can pack a lunch and launch her boat at a minute's notice and be on any one of a thousand secluded beaches in no time at all—a journey she takes often.

Unlike me, Clover did not grow up on the islands or even near a beach. Quite the contrary, she was raised in Michigan. Clover was a young woman before she saw the ocean for the first time, but one look was all it took. She was hooked. She moved her life—lock, stock, and barrel—to Florida and vowed to never be more than a breath away from the water.

I clearly remember one of my trips to visit her there. We spent a lazy, sun-drenched day combing the beaches looking for shells, sitting in the sand at the water's edge, and munching on tortilla chips and her delicious homemade salsa. Clover would sort through my finds, naming each one and telling me about the critter that built it. Every once in a while, she'd pick up an especially pretty specimen, bring it to her lips, and softly kiss it. Then with all the strength she could muster, she'd throw it as far out into the ocean as she could. Puzzled, I asked her what she was doing with my treasures. With a twinkle in her eye and a sparkle in her voice, she said, "That one was much too beautiful to take home. It belongs here."

I wanted that day to never end. As we packed up our gear to head home, the sun began to sink into the horizon in a fiery display of color that left us both breathless. As the last sliver

of sun sizzled into the ocean, Clover stood up and clapped her hands with an ovation that was worthy of only such a masterpiece. I watched her totally immersed in this vision of God's handiwork and vowed I would keep this memory forever.

It has been said that life should not be measured by how many breaths we take, but rather by how many moments take our breath away. In that breathless moment on the beach, I came to realize that Clover has a gift that many of us spend a lifetime searching for—love and excitement for something, an understanding and appreciation for it, and, most importantly, the ability to make the time to enjoy it. Her immeasurable passion for a life she created for herself in Florida makes her "She Who Loves the Beach."

Suzy Toronto

Clover's Super-Simple Salsa

3 medium ripe tomatoes, chopped
2 medium jalapeño peppers, diced
1 medium sweet onion, chopped
1 green or yellow pepper, chopped
3 celery stalks, chopped
¼ cup ketchup
Minced fresh garlic, to taste
Salt and pepper

Mix everything together, and let it sit in the fridge—overnight is best.

Now pack your shelling basket, grab a bag of tortilla chips, and head to the beach! Life doesn't get any better than this!

PS: We like to drink ginger ale with our chips and salsa on the beach. We don't know why—it's just one of those spontaneous rituals. But it tastes soooo good together. Try it!

She Who
Stands for Something

She chooses the purity
of truth over popularity… every time.
Possessing the moral courage
to make her action consistent
with her knowledge of right and wrong,
she knows that the choices she makes today
will shape her into the woman
she will be tomorrow.

This woman's life defines such words
as love, forgiveness, charity,
service, compassion, and godliness,
for she knows who she is
and what she believes.

Her integrity is founded on unswerving principle.
She is beyond reproach,
and her courage is unsurpassed
as she carries the banner of truth.

Everyone knows
she stands for something.

She Who Stands for Something

It's always admirable when someone has the courage to stand in the face of adversity. When that person is a seventeen-year-old girl, it's downright impressive. Such is the case of Cindy.

Cindy was the student-body president of the largest high school in the state of Idaho. She was a bit overwhelmed by the challenge, but that didn't slow her down. She had an agenda, and she was determined to see it through.

For as long as any of the faculty could remember, the Pledge of Allegiance had not been recited at the school by the student body. No one quite knew when it had been removed from the morning announcements, but Cindy—whose blood runs red, white, and blue—decided it was time to put it back in. All she wanted to do was start each morning's announcements with the Pledge of Allegiance.

With absolutely no support from her peers and only skeptical smirks from the faculty, she got approval from the principal.

The very next morning, with her heart racing in her chest, she threw her shoulders back, held her head high, and walked into the school office. Adjusting the microphone of the PA system, she took a deep breath and asked everyone in the school to stand up where they were and join her in the Pledge of Allegiance. With the office staff looking on, Cindy firmly placed her right hand over her heart and recited the pledge. No one joined her— no teachers, no students, not even her vice president. Everyone thought it was a dead deal, never to happen again.

The next morning there were more than a few raised eyebrows when she once again recited the pledge—all by herself. And this continued day after day. Weeks turned into months. Eventually the chatter of the morning rush began to hush, and although no one would join her in her recitation, the students and faculty courteously quit talking during the pledge. After a few more weeks, some students started to stand and look up toward the speaker and listen. One by one, they started to place their hands over their hearts in silent respect. By the beginning of the next semester, it was obvious to the faculty that Cindy was not going to give up. They began to join her, and by year's end, the pledge was once again an everyday, patriotic ritual at the school.

The local press heard about Cindy's efforts and the school's miraculous transformation, and suddenly they wanted to interview her. Articles were written and photos were taken. She was a local heroine. But Cindy didn't revel in the glory. Her goal was to reinstill in the student body a basic patriotic love,

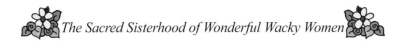

allegiance, and respect for our country. It wasn't easy—standing up for what's right seldom is—but that's exactly what she did.

This past July, almost twelve years since Cindy made her courageous stand, I watched her gently hand her young daughter an American flag to wave at the Fourth of July parade. As she lovingly explained to the child how important it is to never let the flag touch the ground and to wave it when the veterans walked by, she touched my heart as well. In that moment, I knew Cindy was teaching her little girl how to be a woman who stands for something too.

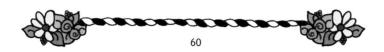

Suzy Toronto

Cindy's Fourth of July Baked Beans

2 tablespoons butter
1 large onion, chopped
1 pound extra-lean ground beef
1 large green pepper, chopped
1 envelope dry onion soup mix
1 cup barbecue sauce
2 15-ounce cans pork and beans with tomato sauce, undrained
½ cup water
2 tablespoons prepared yellow mustard
1 15-ounce can kidney beans
1 15-ounce can garbanzo beans
2 teaspoons vinegar

Preheat oven to 300 degrees.

In a large Dutch oven, brown onion and ground beef in butter. Do not brown the green pepper—it will make it bitter. Now add everything else, including the green pepper. Bake uncovered for 2 hours.

These baked beans are so good, family and friends have been known to pile them on a bun and eat them like a sloppy joe.

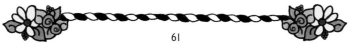

She Whom I Lean On

Sometimes you just can't go it alone.
The challenge is too much to bear.
There's no easy way out.

You don't need advice…
you know what needs to be done.

So you turn to a
rare and precious friend…
someone you trust
who's never let you down.
Through thick and thin,
ever standing in the wings to help,
she listens, consoles, and supports.
She's your personal sounding board.
Best of all, she knows you well enough
to say what needs to be said,
yet she's smart enough
to know what not to say.

Bottom line: she's always there—
arms extended, heart open.
And you thank God
you have somebody to lean on.

She Whom I Lean On

Sandy and I met over twenty years ago, and we were instant soul mates. We had very little in common really. For some reason, this is a recurring theme with my close friends. I tend to seek out people so different from myself that they fill in the gaps where I run short.

When we met, Sandy had four children and a station wagon. I was childless with a flashy sports car. She was a stay-at-home mom, and I was a full-time working girl. Nevertheless, we bonded. It might have been that both of us were night owls married to early-to-bed, early-to-rise husbands. (What a boring schedule!) At 2:00 a.m. she'd look out her window, and seeing my lights still on, she'd flit across the lawn like a fairy in a bubblegum-pink tricot nightgown. She'd bring gooey, sticky pecan rolls—or sometimes a whole pan of her famous almond pastries—that we'd devour in minutes. Of course, we were both always on a diet, but we figured if we didn't tell anyone, it didn't count. We'd talk past the wee hours of the morning, playing beauty shop and doing our nails. We told each other

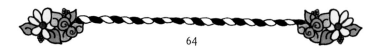

things we've never told another living soul. She has enough dirt on me to blackmail me forever!

As the years went by, we each struggled to find our own path. We took turns talking and listening. Ultimately, we became each other's safe refuge. In times of crisis, I escaped to her and she escaped to me. The best part was I never had to explain myself to her. She accepted me at face value. She knew I'd work through the problems I faced, just as I knew she'd work through hers. Our relationship comes as close to unconditional acceptance as anything I've ever known.

Solving our own problems without any outside advice was the foundation of our relationship. We both knew deep in our hearts that we possessed the intuition and power to make the right choices based on principle. We both came to realize that the light of truth was within us and we'd eventually sort out our challenges. But this didn't mean we had to face our challenges alone. Having each other to lean on until we could stand on our own was not a sign of weakness. It was quite the opposite. I saw it as a sign of strength that we could admit our shortcomings and seek the support we needed. It's been through overcoming our weaknesses that Sandy and I have become strong, resilient women. In the end, we are both thankful for the adversity we've faced.

Now over twenty years later, I remember with fondness that time of my life when my friendship with Sandy was forged. Although

we don't talk as often as we used to, our bond is still there, stronger than ever. And I still know I always have someone to lean on!

I love you, Sandy!

Sandy's Almond Puff Pastry

"Puff" refers to the pastry, not your waistline... I just want to clarify that!

1 cup (2 sticks) chilled butter, divided
2 cups flour, divided
2 tablespoons ice water
1 cup water
1 teaspoon almond extract
3 eggs

Preheat oven to 350 degrees.

Cut ½ cup butter into 1 cup flour. Sprinkle 2 tablespoons ice water over and mix with fork.

Round dough into ball; divide in half. On an ungreased cookie sheet, pat each half into 12" by 13" strips.

In a medium saucepan, heat remaining butter and 1 cup water to rolling boil. Remove from heat, and quickly stir in almond extract

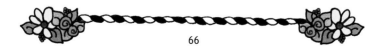

and 1 cup flour. Stir vigorously over low heat until a ball forms.
Remove from heat. Beat in eggs and stir until smooth.

Divide in half and spread over the two pastry strips.

Bake for 60 minutes. Cool before glazing.

Glaze

1½ cups powdered sugar
2 tablespoons butter
1½ teaspoons almond extract
1-2 tablespoons milk or cream, as needed for smooth consistency
For garnish: chopped almonds or walnuts

Mix all the ingredients together in a small bowl. Frost pastries
with glaze, and sprinkle with chopped almonds or walnuts.

Best eaten at 2:00 a.m. in your nightgown and shared with
a girlfriend.

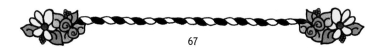

They Who Are Sisters

Together, you've been through it all…
growing pains, sibling rivalry, teasing,
clothes swapping, boys, family vacations…
even Mom's "Tuna Surprise."

You didn't choose each other…
fate took care of that.
Bound by blood and upbringing,
you've shared experiences
that have shaped you into the women you are.
Alike in many ways, yet so different,
sometimes you question whether
you came from the same gene pool,
much less the same planet.
But an eternal bond that transcends friendship
fuses you together
with a never-ending, unquestionable love.

Bottom line…
she really is the one you can call
at four in the morning.
She really is the one who's always there…
through thick and thin, no matter what.
And you thank God you have a sister.

They Who Are Sisters

I have only one sibling, a sister, Cathy, who is five years older than I am. Both Cathy and I have the same biological parents, but that's where the similarities end. We are quite opposite in every way. Our relationship as children was rocky to say the least. She was the big sister I worshiped; I was the bratty kid sister who got in her way. I always laugh when women say they hope to have two baby girls so they can grow up as friends and playmates. I used to think, "I chose my playmates as a child, and I never would have chosen Cathy." We were too different in age and taste. But we are sisters. Forever bound with an immeasurable strength that no one can break, I find it hard to put into words what she means to me.

Cathy and I have a great relationship as adults. She really is the one person I can call at four in the morning. I can't think of anything I would ever ask of her that she would deny me. Cathy is the most giving and charitable person I know. Even with all the loving things she has done for me over the years,

until she reads this, I doubt she knows which one made the biggest impact on me—the one thing that assured me she was truly my sister and that, through thick and thin, she would always be there.

When we were just twelve and seven years old respectively, Mom was diagnosed with a rare and very aggressive form of cancer. Her prognosis was not good. She endured horrible radiation treatments and aggressive surgery in an attempt to eradicate the cancer. She was very ill. It was a traumatic time for all of us. We had just moved to a little island in the middle of the Pacific with no family or friends around to help us. My father was just starting a new job and spent all his time either working or at my mother's side. Struggling to hold it all together, Dad used to make us a huge pot of the most disgusting hamburger soup. He obviously thought we liked it, because as soon as we got rid of it, he'd make another big pot. If I close my eyes I can still smell the nasty stuff to this day! He'd leave it in the refrigerator for us to warm up and eat all week.

We would come home from school to an empty house, and Cathy would fix dinner. We both agreed that the soup was unbearable, so we'd ladle out a healthy portion—a believable amount that looked like what we would have consumed— and rinse it down the sink. Then she'd make the only thing she knew how to cook: Minute Rice with a can of Franco-

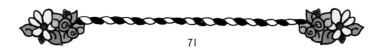

American chicken gravy poured over the top. To this day that strange combination is still one of my favorite comfort foods.

As my eighth birthday was fast approaching, I didn't know if there would be a celebration or not. After all, birthdays were a "Mom thing," and Mom wasn't there. But my dear sister, Cathy, the one I pestered, annoyed, and bothered over the years, didn't let me down. She baked me the most glorious birthday cake I'd ever seen. I'm sure in reality it wasn't much, but to me it was better than anything Martha Stewart could ever come up with. It was chocolate with pink frosting literally sliding off the sides. We invited two neighborhood children to come over, and they all sang "Happy Birthday" to me. It's a memory so imprinted in my mind and in my heart that I will never forget it.

I once heard someone say that we never know when we are creating a memory for someone else. Growing up with siblings is all about memories. Those individual events give commonality to our relationships—both the good and the gut-wrenching things we endure that make us family. They expose our most intimate side and allow us to fuse permanently into each other's heart.

To this day, my birthday is my favorite day of the year. I never fret over getting older. My birthday is a celebration

of more than just my birth. It is a celebration of the event that bound Cathy to me forever.

Cathy, come to think of it, I would choose you as my friend!

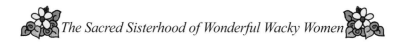

Cathy's Famous Carrot Cake

Cathy's cake-baking skills have improved somewhat over the years, to say the least. So much so that she is famous all over the South for this carrot cake recipe. I often call to see if she has one sitting in the fridge and beg a slice from her. If you like carrot cake, this one is worth every calorie and blowing a diet for. Make it several days before you want to eat it, as it truly improves with age.

Makes one 3-layer cake

4 eggs
2 cups sugar
1⅓ cups oil
2 cups flour
2 teaspoons baking soda
2 teaspoons ground cinnamon
4 cups shredded carrots
¾–1 cup chopped walnuts
1–1¼ cups flaked coconut

Preheat oven to 350 degrees. Grease three 8- or 9-inch cake pans.

In a large mixing bowl, beat eggs with an electric mixer. Add sugar and beat. Add oil and beat. Stir in dry ingredients. Fold in carrots, walnuts, and coconut.

Bake for 40 to 50 minutes. Cake should be firm to touch. Let cool before frosting.

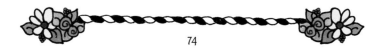

Frosting

½ cup (1 stick) butter, softened
12 ounces cream cheese
1¼ pounds powdered sugar

In a medium bowl, beat butter and cream cheese together. Mix in powdered sugar. Frost completely cooled cake with frosting.

Now here is the really hard part: you have to put the cake in the refrigerator and wait for the cake to "ripen" for at least 48 hours before you cut into it. Trust me, it's a whole different cake without the wait. The cake gets denser and moister with your patience! By the way, the first time you make this, if you can convince everyone to wait 48 hours, you'll probably still need to post 24-hour guards for 2 days to fight off attackers trying to sneak a bite before it's ready. This cake is, without exception, the most wonderful thing I've ever put in my mouth!

Keep it refrigerated.

She Who Loves
to Grow Stuff

It's plan, plant, pleasure, and play...
not work.
No words clearly express
the depth of the contentment
found in the shelter of her garden.
She just isn't happy
unless there's dirt under her fingernails.
For her, no greater peace can be found
than in her garden.
From veggies to violets,
lavender to larkspur,
miracles are an everyday experience
in this partnership
between gardener and God.

She Who Loves to Grow Stuff

I can paint, draw, cook, and sew. But tell a lush, green philodendron that I'm going to plant-sit for the week, and the poor thing will wilt in minutes and give up the ghost. I don't know why, because I love plants. I just don't seem to have what it takes to keep them alive. But that's okay. I'm the kind of person who makes it possible for plant-tending services to stay in business.

My friend Julie doesn't have that problem. From her tattered straw hat to the tip of her little green thumb, Julie loves to grow stuff. It doesn't matter what—just stuff. Whether her nurturing care is needed in the veggie patch or the rose garden, the herb pots or the bulb box, she's a happy camper as long as she's playing in the dirt. She's even content to sit and watch the grass grow. When I drop in for a visit, I look for her in the garden before knocking on the door. And more often than not, there she is.

On a beautiful fall day, I found her out back picking raspberries. With the promise of a generous bowl of raspberries and cream, I joined her in the laborious task. Of course, I would pop one in my mouth for every one that I dropped in the pail until I

absolutely could eat no more. The sweet raspberries were not only a delight to eat, but they stained my fingers with a rosy blush that smelled wonderful. Sad that I didn't have my own raspberry bushes, I went into my usual lament of how I wished I could grow stuff. Julie sighed. She put her hand on the top of her hat, looked up at the brilliant blue sky and said, "Oh Suz, I don't grow anything. I just tend it for Him."

As I left Julie's house that day, my arms filled with a bouquet of fresh-cut flowers and a bottle of her raspberry freezer jam, I thought about her simple, yet profound statement. How often do we take credit for things that are really not ours to claim? Although I don't think I am a terribly boastful person, looking back now, I see that just maybe I have claimed credit for things that were not entirely my doing. I can't tell you how many times I've finished a task, a talk, a project, or a major event and flippantly remarked what a miracle it was that it all worked out—only to then continue on with my life, never truly acknowledging that, in fact, it really was an honest-to-goodness, bona fide miracle!

That year, I spent a lot of time in Julie's garden, and it taught me so much. What a lovely way God has of gently hitting me over the head and knocking some sense into me. As I worked that raspberry patch and harvested her crab-apple tree later that year, I thought how the whole process of a garden taught me about the continuing circle of life. When planting seeds, I had to exercise faith that they would grow. By acting on that faith and nurturing them, they bloomed into magnificent works

of nature. Even as the tiny seedlings took root in the cracks and crevices of her garden wall and walkways, I learned that sometimes I, too, need to bloom where I am planted, despite my circumstances. And when the garden reached its fullness that fall, it taught me that, like all living things, the cycle comes full circle as the garden is eventually turned back into the ground.

I'm going to keep trying to grow stuff or at least tend to the growing things around me. That includes my family, friends, and loved ones—and, oh yeah, that little green succulent clinging for dear life on my front porch.

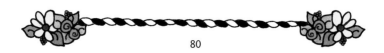

Suzy Toronto

Julie's Berry Heaven

1 cup whipping cream
Sugar, to taste (I use about 2 tablespoons)
2 cups custard-style vanilla yogurt
1 8-inch angel food cake, cut into 1-inch cubes
1 cup fresh blueberries
1 cup sliced fresh strawberries
1 cup fresh raspberries

You can use any assortment of berries—just make sure you have 3 cups.

Beat whipping cream and sugar in chilled medium bowl with electric mixer on high speed until stiff peaks form. Fold in yogurt.

Place cake pieces in large bowl; fold in yogurt mixture. Gently mix berries together in medium bowl.

Spoon half of the cake mixture into a 9-inch springform pan; press firmly in pan with rubber spatula. Top with half of the berries. Repeat with remaining cake mixture and berries. Cover and refrigerate at least 4 hours or overnight.

Run metal spatula carefully along side of dessert to loosen. Remove side of pan. Cut dessert into wedges.

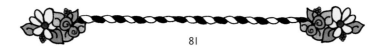

She Who
Gives of Herself

Her arrival announces,
"Clear all decks; help is here."

Sweeping aside protests of indifference,
she sets in motion her gifts
as a labor of love.
Task completed, barely stopping
to breathe in a heartfelt "Thanks,"
she scurries out into the world content.

Onward, ever onward in selfless sacrifice
with never a selfish thought,
blessed is her name...
She Who Gives of Herself.

She Who Gives of Herself

I have always been a "can do" girl—the kind of woman that people can turn to when they need help. I can assess a problem fairly quick and then either give them aid or point them in the right direction. Now don't get me wrong—I'm no angel of mercy, but I've done my share of charity work. However, do you ever wonder where people like me turn when we need help? Well, I'll tell you—nowhere. We suffer in silence, not wanting to burden anyone else. After all, we really don't *need* anything. We can figure out how to get through the crisis of the moment. At least that's what I always thought, until I encountered the tender, loving care of Kim.

I can't honestly say Kim and I are close friends—more like close acquaintances. We each run with a different crowd of wonderful, wacky women, and we have never really socialized with each other that much. Some of our kids are the same ages, and our paths have crossed more than just a few times over the last twelve years. We've both been involved in the same church and community projects.

Suzy Toronto

It was about one such project that Kim phoned me to solicit help. The day she called I was flat out in bed with the worst cold or flu I've ever had—one of those bugs you think could kill you and you're afraid it won't. I was feverish and miserable, and every ounce of my body was aching, but when she called, my "can do" mentality kicked in. I tried to sound upbeat and focus on what she was saying. However, I finally conceded that I was just too sick to help. She asked if I needed any help. I told her, "I'm fine, Kim. I just need a little rest."

At some point the cold/flu meds kicked in, and I passed out into a drugged sleep. I awoke sometime later to hear my front door opening. (I never lock the house. Come to think of it, I don't even know where a key is.) I called out, expecting it to be my husband or one of the kids. It was Kim. As I staggered to the kitchen, she was placing a large pot of vegetable soup on the stove. She shooed me back into bed, straightened my bedding, got me fresh water, and tenderly laid her hand across my forehead to feel my temperature. I didn't *need* the help, but I can't even begin to describe how good it made me feel to know that somebody cared—that someone knew I was sick and miserable. My body would have survived without her, but my heart was eternally soothed by her compassion. Later that evening when my husband brought me a bowl of Kim's delicious soup, it was not only my body that was nourished, but my soul as well. Days later when I called to thank her for her kindness, she shrugged it off and then chastised me for almost denying her the blessing of serving me. I had been blessed with the greatest gift anyone could give—the gift of self.

Kim had exalted her simple existence to the "errands of angels," lifting me in the process. It would have been so easy for Kim to accept my refusal for help. Instead she listened with her heart. I was in need, whether I knew it or not, and I was blessed by her tender care.

Kim wasn't trying to be Mother Teresa, but for me that day, she was. Like Mother Teresa, she wasn't taking on the burdens of the entire world, but rather tending to the needs of one sick friend—one pot of soup at a time.

It's been years since that nasty flu bug took me for a spin, but just yesterday I had to have surgery to deal with painful varicose veins in my legs. It's really no big deal. It hurts and I'm feeling a little "moonie" (a Toronto family word for when we want some sympathy). But don't worry about me. I'm fine. I've got my leg propped up with soft down pillows, and once again I'm sipping on a steaming hot cup of Kim's soothing, nurturing, vegetable soup!

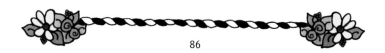

Suzy Toronto

Kim's Make-You-Feel-Good Soup

2 tablespoons olive oil
2 cups chopped onions or leeks
1 cup thinly sliced celery
2 teaspoons Italian seasoning
Coarse salt and ground pepper
3 14½-ounce cans reduced-sodium vegetable or chicken broth
1 28-ounce can diced tomatoes, with juice
1 tablespoon tomato paste
3 cups water
8 cups mixed fresh vegetables, such as carrots, corn, green beans,
    lima beans, peas, potatoes, and zucchini (cut larger vegetables
    into smaller pieces)

Heat oil in a large stockpot over medium heat. Stir in onions or leeks, celery, and Italian seasoning. Season with salt and pepper. Cook, stirring frequently, until onions are translucent and the house begins to smell wonderful, about 5 to 8 minutes.

Add broth, tomatoes and their juice, tomato paste, and water to pot; bring mixture to a boil. Reduce heat to a simmer. Cook uncovered for 20 minutes.

Add mixed vegetables to pot, and return to a simmer. Cook uncovered until vegetables are tender, 20 to 25 minutes. Adjust seasoning with salt and pepper, as desired. Let cool before storing.

Divide the soup into two separate pots, and take one of them to a neighbor or friend who needs a little TLC.

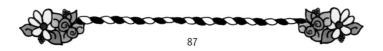

She Who
Seeks a Better Way

She used to believe "things" mattered.
She spent her time collecting,
counting, and storing "stuff."
Then it happened…
the epiphany that changed her life.
Whether it was the revelation
that less is more
or that she simply began to feel
her "stuff" owned her,
she finally got it:
the secret to true happiness lies
not in accumulating more,
but in wanting less!
Setting aside the things of the world,
her once cluttered and congested life
gave way to tranquility,
order, and peace.
Cleaning out the closets of her life
gave her twice as much space
for what matters most:
the love of her family,
the joy of dear friends,
and the irrepressible sound
of her own laughter.

A Short Note…
I'm often asked which Wonderful Wacky Woman painting
is my favorite. Although from time to time different images
are closer to my heart, overall I'd have to say it's "She
Who Seeks a Better Way." I painted it on my forty-fifth
birthday on location in Albuquerque, New Mexico, during
the International Balloon Festival. There is no doubt
the colors were influenced by the thousand balloons that
ascended that crisp fall morning… obviously in honor of
my special day!

She Who Seeks a Better Way

About three years ago, a bunch of us wild, wacky
women took a girls-only trip to my old stomping
grounds in Hawaii. We decided to splurge and rent a
top-notch, five-star condo. The brochure bragged that
the accommodations came fully stocked with everything
we could possibly need to live, cook, and relax in the
nurturing, balmy environment of the islands. Upon our
arrival, we oohed and aahed, pinching ourselves at how

lucky we were to have gotten such luxury digs. Like any curious females, the first thing we did was run around like crazy women, opening up every cupboard, drawer, and closet to assess the full scope of what our combined money had bought for the month. We were inspired by the simplicity of the place, the energy of the rooms, the layout of the kitchen and lanai, and the unbelievable view of the pearly white sand and pounding surf. In the coming days, we reveled in the soothing calm of our sanctuary. We all felt burdens lifted and a rejuvenation of our bodies, minds, and spirits. Our cups were truly filled to overflowing.

About a week into the trip, one by one, we began to come up for air. We had each set our own pace and really begun to absorb the energy that one can only get in the islands. We took turns with the cooking and light housekeeping, which seemed effortless. Despite the luxury surroundings and gourmet meals we were preparing, everything seemed to be a cinch to maintain. Each time we returned to our condo after an ethereal day at the beach or an afternoon of touring, we each felt the same relaxing, uncluttered energy that we all wanted to take home with us. As we lounged on the lanai of our tropical oasis nibbling Kooky Koconut Kookies, which we had discovered at a quaint little hole-in-the-wall bakery, the epiphany hit us. The main difference

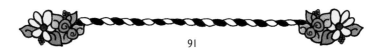

between this tranquil retreat and our own over-saturated habitats was the lack of stuff. Unlike our homes, which were bursting at the seams with the clutter of day-to-day living, useless collections, and unused gadgets, this condo was equipped for efficiency. Filled with only the bare essentials, it had everything we needed—not just to survive, but to really live well. True, it lacked the emotional history of photos and keepsakes that gives our homes a rich, well-lived patina, but we all decided that a little of this bare-bones efficiency could drastically improve our lives.

We made a pact to go home and unclutter our lives. As we boarded the plane a month later, we were women on a mission. Our goal was to create a peaceful, uncluttered energy in our own homes, yet still have them reflect each of us personally.

Some of us were better at it than others.

Chloe was a natural. Her theory had always been "when in doubt, throw it out." It was no surprise to any of us that no sooner had she gotten home than she began to dig out and throw out like there was no tomorrow. In no time at all, her already minimalist modern home took on the uncluttered energy of a model home, accented by only the most basic of personal mementos. Voted by

all the wild, wacky women as the least likely to need the digging out in the first place, she was the first to fly through it. We all hated her!

Chris took to the task with a different approach. She began by educating herself with every self-help book ever written on the skill of organizing clutter. Not willing to give up her "I just might need it someday" mentality, Chris reached a happy compromise. Instead of tossing things out, she organized her junk so at least she didn't have to trip over it every day. It made her happy. She is now the self-proclaimed "Queen of Labeled Plastic Storage Bins," with a whole room in her house dedicated to storing them. It works for her—and that's what matters.

Angie, who has always been better at denial than reality, lost the vision of her quest right away. After cleaning house, she simply rented a storage unit for $125 per month to put all her stuff in. She now claims to be paying about $3,000 every year to store $600 worth of junk. But it's out of her house and out of her mind, and she doesn't have to deal with it. Like Chris, it works for her.

As for me, I faced a challenge. I raised a houseful of kids in my home in northern Idaho. The rooms were chock-full of memories in the form of photos, children's

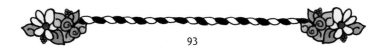

artwork, outgrown toys, and boxes of past-their-prime handmade dresses. I had knickknacks that represented not only my own collections, but gifts and family items that had been handed down through decades. The decluttering process was accelerated by the fact that we were putting our home on the market, and a good thinning out was desperately needed. My method was to dump everything in the middle of the room and then return to their places only the things I was destined to keep. With a mountain of a mess before me, I climbed to the top of the heap and dug in. Amid the treasures was a ton of stuff I couldn't believe I'd kept to begin with. I sorted the items into separate boxes for each child— boxes that were mail ready so I could easily take them to the post office. The pile for Goodwill was the biggest. For some reason, giving things to a good cause eased the separation anxiety. After a couple of weeks, the house took on a new glow. With closets cleaned and organized, my life was less congested and far easier to maintain.

The place looked its best in years—and it sold. With the move upon us and the cost of shipping at sixty-five cents per pound, I suddenly looked at what was left quite differently. My earthly possessions were just things—the emotion wasn't attached to the objects but to my heart. I didn't need to possess an object to keep the memory. I asked myself, "If all these things burned to the ground tomorrow, would I lose the memories or would it really

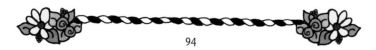

change my life?" I did the hardest letting go in history and packed it all off to charity. With a journal at my side, I made notes as the stuff jogged memories, omitting those that I no longer wanted to harbor. With only the bare essentials and my most treasured keepsakes, we moved three-thousand miles away to our new home.

As I reflect on this major time of letting go of stuff in my life, I've come to several conclusions. First, letting go of the junk in our lives is not limited to tangible things. Emotional baggage is just as heavy as the boxes of unnecessary and unwanted stuff that I shipped off to Goodwill. So I decided to toss out all the negative emotions I'd been carrying around for years as well. Leaving behind the memories of illness, tension, and conflict, I chose only to keep the lessons learned. The most significant was keeping the joy and celebration of my dearest friend Candy's life—not the pain of her illness and death. Thus, I had more time, space, and energy to fill my life with the new adventures of my move to the Southeast.

The rest of the wild, wacky women fell somewhere between Chloe, who got rid of everything, and Chris and Angie, who simply shifted it all around.

As for me, I still catch myself collecting and hanging on to stuff. But now, more aware of what I'm doing than ever,

I'm committed to only keeping those most cherished items in my heart and in my journal and to giving the mementos to my children and friends. Cleaning out the closets of my life both physically and mentally was one of the most productive things I ever did.

Now as I munch on the freshly baked Kooky Koconut Kookies I just made, my mind drifts back to that balmy, tropical retreat that inspired me to realize that less is more and I am not the accumulation of my stuff.

I finally got it!

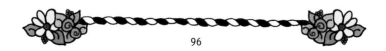

Suzy Toronto

Kooky Koconut Kookies
from the Ohana Bakery

We talked the bakery out of this recipe. They could hardly refuse with five wacky women making such a fuss. They were happy just to get us out the door.

1 14-ounce package flaked coconut
1 14-ounce can sweetened condensed milk
3 teaspoons vanilla extract
1 teaspoon almond extract
½ cup (1 stick) butter (the real stuff), softened
½ cup vegetable shortening
¾ cup granulated sugar

¾ cup packed brown sugar
2 large eggs
2 cups all-purpose flour
1 teaspoon baking powder
½ teaspoon baking soda
¼ teaspoon salt
1 cup macadamia nuts (optional)

Preheat oven to 375 degrees.

In a medium bowl, mix first four ingredients. Set aside.

In a large bowl, beat next four ingredients with an electric mixer until fluffy. Add eggs and continue beating. Add flour, baking powder, baking soda, and salt. Mix well. Gently fold coconut mixture into the batter mixture and add nuts, if desired.

Drop rounded tablespoons of dough onto greased cookie sheet, leaving about 2 inches between cookies. Bake cookies for 12 to 15 minutes. Watch closely so as not to burn them. We like them golden and chewy but not burned.

Kick off your shoes, put on your shades, and eat three of these as fast as you can!

She Who Has Arrived

She used to hate birthdays.
She just wanted to stay twenty-nine forever.
But then one day she realized that
aging really isn't
about getting older…
it's about growing.
And, oh, how she had grown!

The wisdom of her years
had taught her
compassion and understanding.
Now she was tranquil and mellow…
more at peace with herself
and those around her.
It was then she realized
that she liked herself a whole lot more
than she ever had before.
She was finally becoming the woman
she always wanted to be.

She Who Has Arrived

I love my birthday. It's always been the best day of the year. You can forget the other holidays, but by gosh, don't ever forget my birthday! It's October 5—okay!?

My friend Cheryl did not share my enthusiasm. She hated her birthday. She would literally go into mourning a month before the big day. And she made sure everyone knew she was miserable. She'd go into this elaborate ritual of losing weight, buying youthful clothes, and trying to look ten years younger. Then, as beautiful as she was, she really got irritating when she started talking about another nip or tuck to cinch up the deception. I think she actually believed that, given enough effort, she could control the aging process, just like she tried to control everything else around her. She wasn't fooling anyone, and she was driving me nuts. Come to think of it, I hated her birthday too!

Then two weeks before her forty-second birthday, she was diagnosed with breast cancer. Talk about a reality check! Suddenly the thought of growing old sounded pretty darn good.

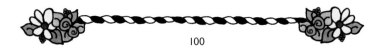

As if a light bulb flickered on in the darkness, Cheryl woke up and realized that growing old was exactly what she wanted. She wanted to be an eighty-year-old woman with silvery white hair and a dozen great-grandchildren at her feet. She wanted to become a sage among women, growing in wisdom, compassion, and understanding. With those thoughts, she channeled all her energy and resources into recovery and set a new course for her life.

It's been eight years since Cheryl's diagnosis. She is cancer-free and finally content with her life. Instead of wasting time on things over which she has no control, she finished her degree in sociology. She also volunteers one day a week at the local food bank and teaches yoga at the community recreation center. As I am getting ready to help her celebrate her half-century birthday next week, I'm taken back to the time when she was obsessed with the things in life and not life itself. She still has a tendency to control things, but now that she's no longer worried about what chocolate might do to her waistline, she called to tell me what kind of cake to make for her party. She can't wait till her fiftieth birthday—and that's okay.

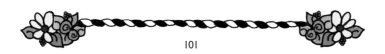

Cheryl's Big 5-0
Southern Chocolate Sour Cream Cake

If you're going to blow a diet, make it worth every bite. This cake is so good that you'll want to invent a birthday just for an excuse to bake it.

¾ cup unsweetened cocoa
1¾ cups sugar, divided
4 large eggs, 3 of them separated
½ cup milk
½ cup (1 stick) butter or margarine
2 cups all-purpose flour, sifted
1 teaspoon baking powder
1 teaspoon baking soda
½ teaspoon salt
1 cup sour cream
1 teaspoon vanilla extract

Preheat oven to 350 degrees.

In a medium saucepan over low heat, mix cocoa, ¾ cup sugar, 1 egg yolk, and milk. Cook, stirring until thickened. Cool.

In a large bowl, cream butter or margarine with an electric mixer until light and fluffy; add remaining 1 cup of sugar, and beat until well blended. Add 1 egg and 2 egg yolks. Mix well.

In a medium bowl, combine flour, baking powder, baking soda, and salt. Stir dry ingredients alternately with sour cream into

batter. Add vanilla and cocoa mixture. Beat remaining 3 egg whites until stiff, and fold into cake batter. Line bottoms of three 8-inch cake pans with wax paper. Pour batter into the pans. Bake for 30 to 35 minutes. Turn out onto racks and peel off wax paper. Cool.

Chocolate Butter Frosting

¾ cup (1½ sticks) butter, softened
1½ pounds powdered sugar (about 6 cups sifted, 4½ cups
    unsifted), sifted
1 dash salt
2 teaspoons vanilla extract
5 ounces (5 squares) unsweetened chocolate, melted
¼ cup sour cream

In a large bowl, cream butter with an electric mixer; gradually add sifted powdered sugar. Add salt, vanilla extract, melted chocolate, and about 3 tablespoons of sour cream. Beat until smooth and spreadable, adding more sour cream if necessary.

Like the carrot cake my sister makes, this Southern sour cream cake is really better chilled overnight. However, if you double the frosting recipe, you can use half on the cake and immediately eat the rest directly out of the bowl to tide you over.